Graham Sessions

Published by: G Sessions, 5 Luxton Court, EX15 1FJ
Imprint: Blurb.co.uk

A view in poetry of the changing world;
The Seasons;
The Technology;
The Environment;
The People;
The Attitudes.

Some things change but little.

Weather Changes

Trees, trees
Their leaves rustle
In the breeze
To break
The silence
In the air.

The wind gathers force
To show no remorse
To the damage it may cause
Everywhere.

Storm, storm
Recently born
Brings with it the rain.
The swollen streams, the mud,
The devastating flood
That serves only to
Bring more pain.

Snow, snow
From the East
Carpets all the land;
But wait!
The Sun is brighter;
And now summer is at hand.

A Field of Dreams

I saw a cloud up in the sky
Drifting slowly
Very high,
Appearing as a great white bird
Flying northward,
Never heard.
A greater image never seen
Save to remind me
Of a dream
I once had of a field of flowers
Freshened from the night time showers,
Now gazing upward
T'ward the sun
And smiling
Each and every one.
But come the sunset,
Come the night
They close their eyes,
Give up the fight
And very slowly start to creep
Into their nightly,
Flowery
Sleep.

Evidence

Evidence forthcoming
From CCTV
Interview the suspect:
"It wasn't me!"

"Please explain these images,"
This question it was asked.
"I called in for a take-away,
Was only walking past."

"We have got some fingerprints,
They match yours right enough."
"They were taken at another time
'Cos I was wearing gloves."

"Another piece of evidence
That we have here 'just for fun'
Is a sample of your DNA
From the handle of the gun."

"Where d'ya get that gun from?"
"I owned it years ago,
But I sold it to another bloke
For his wild western show."

"Then how is it when tested
There was residue on your skin
From firing this gun recently?
Now confess. We'll take you in."

"Ask the chip shop owner,
He'll confirm just what I said."
"That will prove quite difficult.
The chip shop owner's dead!"

Birds

We put out seeds,
Fat blocks too.
The sound of silence
Echoes through
The atmosphere.
We wait so long
To hear the cheerful
Birds in song.
They come at last
And rest among
The gift of morsels
Firmly hung.
They start to sing
Their Merry song
And feed as any day
'Ere long.
And later on
They all retire
To branches high
And even higher
To rest a while
And keep their nests
Safe from all
Unwelcome guests.
Later on
They come once more
To raid the
Ever hanging store.

Kaleidoscope

All the primary colours
And secondary colours too;
Changing patterns randomly
Available to view.
A mix of irregularity
And inversions lateral
Display the wealth of colours
In forms which are
Collateral.

A simple mechanism
And mirrors set just right
With multicoloured crystals
Produce a stunning sight.
But the enquiring visitor
Who peers into the void
Is unaware that all are just
Some chips of celluloid.

You Absorb Me
(Love from a Distance)

You absorb me.
When I see you
You are mine
But I am not yours.
Alone;
I want you,
Ache for you.
I remain alone.

Your hair falls like the sunset:
As a deep orange glow.
Your skin:
A pale contrast;
Delicate,
Soft.

I want to hold you;
I want to meet those lips
Which I have only seen
From afar.
I need to be close to you;
To touch;
To feel your warmth.

I know how you feel:
Nothing for me
And I shall never belong to you
But you will always belong to me
In my heart,
My mind.

You are everything that can be;
As near perfection as
Anything could be;
As near to me as you would be
But as far from me as I would wish,
Or further.

You absorb me.
When I see you
You are mine
But I am not yours.
Alone;
I want you,
Ache for you.
I remain alone
Until the day that changes.

When I was a Little Boy

From when I was a little boy,
Innocent of face,
I used to race my mother
Or rather she gave chase,
Because I was so naughty
And ran out from the house.
Mostly I hid quietly
Just like a little mouse.

Down alleyways oft' I wandered
And hid behind the sheds;
I climbed upon the bunkers
And tore my shorts to shreds.
Mostly, though I played inside
With games upon the table,
Or even with the cars I had
Upon the floor when I was able.

One day I was presented
With a present from Granddad.
It was a Hornby Dublo train set:
The biggest present that I had.
Many hours I did pass
With my brand new Duchess class,
Racing around the oval track
Very, very, very fast.

I bought more points and sidings
And coal wagons and all
And two more locomotives
And carriages to haul.
But one day I had to stop
And couldn't buy any more
Because my model railway
Covered all the floor.

Many years then passed
And I grew up and went away.
My train set rested in its box
Until the judgement day.
I sold all of my layout:
Buildings, track and trains
And saved the twenty pounds or so
'Till it became of use again.

When approaching old age
Construction began again.
I looked forward to the time when I
Could run another train.
I built and built each weekend;
Spent little time away
And my very humble train set
Became a model railway.

Images of You

I gaze into my memory
From time to time
To see what I can find.

I see trees and birds,
Steam locomotives on ancient tracks;
But motorways abound;
They multiply:
Clearing out the old
And replacing them with things that won't last
Forever.

Plastic everywhere,
Mostly useless
And unnecessary
And for which
No one
Takes responsibility;
But they still make it
And take no responsibility.

A milkman on his daily round;
A baker and a grocer too
Wend their ways though the streets,
Stopping where people queue,
To sell their wares.

I gaze into my memory
From time to time
To see what I can find.

I see people turning out the old and valuable
And long lasting
To buy in the new
And cheap
And short lived.

Fashion!
Changes often.
Unnecessary.
Rubbish tips of old electronics
Not recycled.
Pollution.

I see also
Images of you.
From the time we met to now
You have never changed.
You are as you were;
As you have ever been
And ever will be.
Images of you.

Memory

Past times
Stir in my brain
Amorphous
Revolving
Resolving
Into clarity
Home
Terrace
School
Divided by sex
Tall railings
Prisoners from contact
Flags waving
Marching
24th May
Empire Day
Later
Semi-detached
Laburnum tree
Helicopters falling
Sweets from mother's friends
And later again
Semi-detached
Concrete garage
Trains
Model and real
Fire

Burnt carpet
Sad
Much later
Detached
Bungalow
Large garden
Vegetables
Freezer
Bus
School
Boys only
Success
University
Education
And
Education
Images
Photographs
Performance
Singing
Acting
Continuing
Then...
Fading
Clouding
Amorphous
Memory

Performance

The race to the theatre:
Breathless from the rush,
Breathless from excitement;
The anticipation.

The dressing room,
The costume,
The foundation applied
Then added
To model
The character
From the bland
Original face.
Then powder
To set the form
From changing
Under the lights.

The wait:
Vocal exercises start
And then the physical.
Warming muscles
And voice
To permit the character
To come alive.

The Green Room
Where waiting continues,
Tension mounts
And time moves slowly
Towards the opening.

"Beginners, please!"
The caller cries
And some arise
To move into the wings.

They wait.
I wait.
The stage is set
And darkens now
To raise the tension
Of the waiting crowd.

Standby!
"Actors on stage please."
The lights grow brighter;
The curtain rises
And Elsie starts her line.
The play has begun.

Cont'd over ...

The interactions start
And every actor
Plays 'his' part.

When the actors are in full flow
And tensions ease;
The characters grow,
The audience responds
And the plot begins
To flow.

o - O - o

After and hour or so
With sweat dripping
And to great applause
The cast takes a bow.
The curtains close
And lights dim and the actors
Leave the stage
And pass
Into grim and dusty wings
Through which they move
To the dressing rooms
At last.

Perception

That which we see
Is not always there.
Statistics that tell us
Facts without care
To explain what's
Behind them:
The truths
And the lies.
The unexplained data
Which create a disguise.

Masked or unmasked
The truth lies somewhere.
People corrupt it
And take not a care.

The media in all of its facets
Remains
The purveyor
Of lies
And bias
Which stains
The honesty
Of information
Revealed.
Maybe the freedom
Of the press should be
Repealed.

Crunch

Crunch!
The actor finishes
A crisp:
A noisy snack
Between the scenes.
The A.D. shouts,
"Quiet on set, please."
And
As the crunch dies away:
"Sound rolling."
"Camera rolling."
And
"Action!"

o - O - o

"Cut!"
"Let's take a look
At the rushes."
The actors relax.
They move off set
To join the crew
And then...
Crunch!
Crunch!
(pause)
Crunch!

Final Curtain

Waiting in the wings
For the final Bow,
The Actors, tension relieved,
Perspiration dripping;
Breathless beings
With energy expended
And limbs tired
Now that the show
Has ended.
Onto the stage
They race:
Everyone knows
Their place;
They come, them all
The audience to face.
Face to Face,
And now,
Tired as they may be,
They take their bow.
Applause, applause.
So thankful now.
0 - O - 0
So the curtain has descended
And the last performance ended.
The actors depart
And say their farewells
And all that remains is silence.

Phone a Friend

There are questions I can't answer:
The real meaning of life:
Sometimes it plays upon my mind;
The questions become rife.

My brain dissolves in many thoughts
Which cannot all be true:
How far does outer space extend?
Is there another you?

Do aliens exist among
The planets and the stars?
Could they ever reach us
From their homes afar?

Is time the same for everyone?
Does it pass at the same rate,
Or is it just a way to put
Our science on a plate?

To serve it to the public
To help them understand
That space is a beginning
And doesn't have an end.

Is the universe a doughnut?
Can you believe it so?

Solitary or entwined
With doughnut number two.

Our time and space continuum:
Will it ever stop?
That phrase suggests it cannot be;
Could it just go 'pop'!

Are there universes parallel?
Is there more than one of me
Living with my other selves
To infinity.

These are questions I can't answer
But they're often in my mind.
Do we believe in what we're told?
Have they sold it to our kind?

If what I think is really so
Then, "What of that?", I ask.
There's no one who can answer me
And take my thoughts to task.

But still I'll keep on trying
To solve it in the end.
I'll probably just write my book
Or maybe phone a friend.

Breathe

I walked for miles it seemed;
Through wood and copse
And fields of flowers
And over hills:
Climbing and descending
And climbing again.

The walk was tiring.
At first
The trees loomed high overhead
As I strode the forest path.
The woodland creatures chattered
And sang
And waited
and ran.

The canopy appeared
As an explosion of stars
As the sunlight
Pierced the treetops
And formed
Dancing Patterns
On the forest floor.

Then out into the open air
Through copse and brush
Which hid the fauna
Living there.

The trees and shrubs
Are thinning now;
No more the shade
Of laden bough.
No more the canopy
Of the stars.

Small trees and bushes
Of many sorts:
Hawthorne, Blackthorn,
Elder too,
Fading now
From distant view.

More to observe
On country floor;
A flowering carpet
And different grasses;
Reveal themselves
As the time passes.

Viper's-Bugloss
Speedwell too
And very soon
Coming into view:
The distant hills.

Cont'd over ...

The ground becomes
Much more uneven:
Up and down,
The path has given
Way to stones
And dusty earth.

The way is now so tiring
To walk at the same pace.
I slow and take a breath.
It's not sensible to race.

Higher now and higher
I climb towards the sky.
My heartbeat getting faster;
The path turns left and I
See in the near distance
The summit. Not far now
Until I reach a place to rest:
A rocky outcrop
Seems the best.

I rest my body,
The climb now done
And gaze around.
The setting sun
Shines o'er the hills
And I can breathe.

Tick Tock

Tick, tock,
The morning light
Shines through the glass
And lends me sight
Of clothes upon
The bedroom floor
Where they were left
The night before.

I rise and stretch
My aching limbs;
Climb from my bed
To take a shower;
Tidy the mess,
Don my clothes
Ready to love
Each waking hour.

With breakfast done
It's half past eight:
Nothing at all
Left on my plate.
So, off to work:
The day begins
And office desks
With constant clatter
Of keyboards making
Electronic chatter.

Cont'd over ...

After four hours
Conversation
Dulls to find
Some relaxation.
Occasional crackles
Of a sandwich packet
Opening replaces
The morning racket.

Tick, tock,
Lunch has ended
Errors in transcripts
And emails amended.
Electronic conversation
Resumes and on my own station
I take some calls:
Some people are nice;
Others not so but
Such is life.

Tick, tock,
The workday has passed
And now the journey
Home at last.

I open my door
And enter the hall,
Take off my coat,
Pick up the mail
And make myself a cup of tea.
I love what each hour has brought for me.

After dinner: on the settee,
I read a book for an hour or three;
A glass of whisky or maybe gin
Never considered by me a sin.
With sleepy eyes and heavy head:
In time I make my way to bed.

I throw my clothes upon the floor,
Set the alarm for morn.
I've loved each hour today has brought
And look towards the dawn.
I rest my head, pull up the sheets
And listen to the clock.
I wonder what it's telling me.
Tick, tock, tick, tock, tick, t...

Nature's Wonder

When I look
Across the garden,
Filled with colour
From plants fresh sprung.
With different shades
And hues aplenty,
I know it's spring.
The year's begun.

In time the flowers
Wilt and others
Burst into life
To fill the space.
Different plants
With different colours,
Each one keen
To show their grace.

Leaves on trees,
Bright green in youth,
Begin to mellow
As they age.
Through the summer
Days they darken
Then seasons turn another page.

Autumn rears its head
September,
Green living walls
And canopies now changed:
Colours turn brown
And gold and russet.
Leaves fall:
Nature's beauty rearranged.

Barren trees
And hedgerows lining
Fields and roadways
Now exposed
To winter winds.
Snowdrifts and Icicles
All shining;
Vistas now all recomposed.

Such is nature's
Wondrous cycle;
Such is nature's
Elegance;
No end
And no beginning.
Such is nature's
Seasons' dance.

Remains

What is here,
And now exists
Will not evermore be so.
It may decay
Or die away
Be it fast or be it slow.

It may be crushed,
It may have melted;
Dissolved into a watery grave;
Heated by the Earth's own furnace
And swallowed up
In Gaia's cave.

We may never know what happens
For a million years or more.
Perhaps beneath the ground we'll find it,
Or beneath the ocean's floor.
One thing that we know is certain -
It will have changed for sure.

From living things and rocks and objects,
Some things natural, some man made,
There will be changes that maintain.
Naturally with Gaia's wealth
And although all things will fade
Particles will still remain.

Epilogue

From the contents and the preface
Through the weighty introduction,
The many pages of the work
Are written in Times Roman.

Sometimes the font is different,
Or in italic or in bold;
Sometimes there is an indent
Or a margin to behold.

But often there aren't changes
In the text at all.
The work is so absorbing,
It really does enthral.

Towards the end in some works
A bibliography is found
And sometimes there's an index
To find your way around.

But following the main text
Where you found yourself agog,
You may find the prose extended
Into an epilogue.